Red Zone

OTHER BOOKS BY KIM GOLDBERG

Ride Backwards on Dragon (2007)

Where to See Wildlife on Vancouver Island (1997)

Vox Populi (1993)

Submarine Dead Ahead! (1991)

The Barefoot Channel (1990)

RED ZONE

Kim Goldberg

Kim Goldberg

Pig Squash Press

Second Printing, November 2009

Library and Archives Canada Cataloguing in Publication

Goldberg, Kim, 1954-
Red zone / Kim Goldberg.

Poems.
ISBN 978-0-9783223-7-3

I. Title.

PS8613.O434R43 2009 C811'.6 C2009-904802-7

The author gratefully acknowledges the financial assistance of the British Columbia Arts Council.

Many of the pieces in ***RED ZONE*** have also appeared in the following magazines and anthologies: *The Capilano Review, Cimarron Review, Event, Prism International, Prairie Fire, The Dalhousie Review, subTerrain, Front, West Coast Line, Our Times, Many Mountains Moving, Rampike, The Arabesques Review, Voices Israel, Ascent Aspirations, Dream Catcher, Lavandería, Tesseracts, Regreen, Rocksalt* and *I Go to the Ruined Place.*

Title font: The Battle Continuez, by Christopher Hansen.
Primary inside text font: GaramondNo4CyrTCYLig, 11 pt.
Cover photo by Kim Goldberg. Author photo by Shirley Goldberg.

This book is printed in Canada on 80 lb. Rolland Enviro 100 made from 100% recycled content.

Written, photographed, designed and lived by Kim Goldberg entirely on location in beautiful downtown Nanaimo, British Columbia.

Pig Squash Press
35 Prideaux Street
Nanaimo, B.C. V9R 2M3 Canada
www.pigsquashpress.com

for all the Leonards of the underpass

CONTENTS

Midway upon the journey of our life
I found myself within a forest dark
For the straightforward pathway had been lost

Dante Alighieri
The Divine Comedy

Urban Planning

Train tracks scrape past the sun-hammered miners'
shacks left over from the last
century. The front side is tarted up
as the Historic Old Quarter. But the backside
holds the story. Just ask the crumbling sunflower
sentries guarding the ass-end
of the Women's Centre. Or the weather-stripped
shiplap on the Bride's Closet next door
luffing like a beaten flag while some gunk
the colour of old blood drips
from a rusty pipe. I know this stuff
because I am now at a sufficiently advanced
stage in my daily rail-walking to support
a head-up gaze at my surroundings without
tumbling into the thorns. Beyond the
bridal store the shaling Occidental
Hotel and Bar prevails like an asylum
for the criminally insane. While across the
tracks a torn quilt pocked with bodily
stains lies splayed on a weedy patch
behind the Thrift Shop – a cardboard box
nightstand totters beside. She will
sleep here again tonight
unless chance finds her at the copshop on
the corner or perhaps in the bed
of someone she meets in the Oxy. And if he's

not too bad, maybe they'll get hitched
and pay a visit to the Bride's Closet (except
that's likely where her problems started – it's all so
cyclotronic). He'll probably keep
spending his nights at the Oxy, coming home
mean, talking fist-speak, till she ducks
out, goes to the Women's Centre, which
will be closed due to funding cuts, so she'll do
some dumpster diving in the donation box
outside the Thrift Shop till she finds another quilt
and a spot to lie.

Instructions

Begin at the beginning and grasp it firmly with the needle-nose pliers supplied. If the beginning is not visible (it may have retreated within its protective cowling during shipping), then begin from wherever you are. You will not need the needle-nose pliers in this case. If you do not know where you are, then begin anyway unless your surroundings bear any resemblance to a zoological display whose occupants have discovered that cages only exist when they can be seen, thus resulting in significant nocturnal liberation activity (and in some unfortunate instances, fur-soaked carnage). Under these circumstances, it is recommended that you limit your beginning to the hours between sunrise and sunset, and that you always carry the spare neural network supplied in the auxiliary tool kit. To read these instructions in another language, please visit the website.

This is the house

This is the house that Kim bought

This is the street in front of the house
that Kim bought

This is the park at the end of the street in front of the house that Kim bought

This is the person who sleeps in the park at the end of the street in front of the house that Kim bought

Inbrief

police

Body discovered in Barsby Park

Police do not suspect foul play behind the death of a man whose body was found in Barsby Park Saturday.

This is the story that ran on the person who sleeps in the park at the end of the street in front of the house that Kim bought

This is the palace built six blocks away from the story that ran on the person who sleeps in the park at the end of the street in front of the house that Kim bought

This is the feeling about the palace built six blocks away from the story that ran on the person who sleeps in the park at the end of the street in front of the house that Kim bought

This is the City's response to the feeling about the palace built six blocks away from the story that ran on the person who sleeps in the park at the end of the street in front of the house that Kim bought

This is the end of the tale of the City's response to the feeling about the palace built six blocks away from the story that ran on the person who sleeps in the park at the end of the street in front of the house that Kim bought

underpass

dewdamp mound of torn sleep
ing bag greasestained jacket pink baby
blanket shapeless landlocked
amoeba of throwaway
rags frozen
heap stucktight to predawn
concrete sky of broken
glass rockabye ursus
minor orion cassiopeia crymeariverof
dimes
glacial galactic supersubatomic
endtime ice-egg
busted and raised to the zeroth degree
minus infinity (plus a bit)
crackhatching ghostly
wisp of virgo
rising

Creation Theory #17

When they come it will be with butterfly nets

And we will be lazy head-bake sunning on a chest of splintered drawers left curbside for free pick-up

And the sky will be chicory blue with a hint of custard off toward Vancouver

And the Northern Hawk-Owl from the evening news will hold an open house in her cheese-puff heart, but we will be too busy to come

And we will wonder (but not for long) about all the toppled recipes behind the stove, wrestling with dust motes and petrified cookie crumbs, defending their reductionist logic to the bitter last

And we will watch ambulances bolt down a cherry-scream path to the riverside park, load frozen éclairs into a see-yourself-shiny vault and speed off

And we will taste cinnamon bark with our prehensile tongues then sharpen pencil stubs and begin to write

And we will likely not notice when the gossamer drops over us

And we may only subliminally regret that we did not
at least try to attend the Northern Hawk-Owl's party

And we will shape a suet pie homunculus for uses to
be determined later

And if a mood should fall in a forest without making a
sound, we will sop it up with super-absorbent paper
towels

Seed

I was out sowing the seeds of revolution in thc clarity
of February's heatless sun when I saw her yarding
on a pipe wrench, trying to pop the head off a
parking meter. Her straw-blonde hair bobbed each time
she jerked the iron bar. I could hear her grunts from thirty
feet away—me and my fistful of pamphlets flogging
existential aphorisms for self-liberation from the Herd Mind.
My entire revolutionary enterprise was invisible
in her hunger-struck fever on this Sunday afternoon
along this empty gut of sidewalk in Nanaimo's battered
core—the so-called "Red Zone"
from which drug dealers are banned (even though
most of them are addicts, and this is where the needle
exchange and homeless shelter and soup kitchen
are located). The private police force hired by
downtown storekeepers was nowhere in sight on this
particular side street. When I could see the grease stain
on her nylon jacket, she woke from her Zen practice, shoved
the wrench inside her coat and retreated to a door stoop,
moulding herself into a faceless heap of thrift-store rags, hidden
in plain sight. Just more anonymous
curbside detritus. As I passed, I wanted to apologize
for intruding, for interrupting her survival, for being so pathetic
as to think I could change anything by peppering
the streets with Sartre, Camus, Thoreau, neatly parsed into
bite-size portions for close-cropped minds. Confronted

by such compression of life, I saw my puny grasp
held no sufficient offering. I glanced but did not gawk
as I passed this primal lump, this uncarved block
of wood, this dark that hoods the light, this nothingness
that will take flight as ten thousand things,
this seed.

BUTTON
FOR
WALK
SIGNAL
WHAT WOULD HAPPEN
if you didn't go
to work today?

Visitation

My mother tells a story
told to her by her grandmother about her ancestors
(my ancestors), those clear-eyed Vikings
peeling back the skin of new worlds, soaking tangled
beards in honey meade, roaring at the sight of shore – No,
that is another story, although still hers (and mine).
This story is of humbler times spent hoeing parsnips
and rutabagas and whatever else would take root and grow
on windblown Danish fjords. And when the day unwrapped
its last buttery strands, the family – layered in wool and
stubborn earth – trudged back to their cobblestone
cottage (I am extrapolating here on likely construction
materials) that had sheltered countless generations of
Knudsens. They trudged back, heads down, path
memorized like drowsy bears lumbering to the
berry patch. (Wait, let's assume they had some joy
in their bony lives – These were sons and daughters of
Vikings, after all. They couldn't possibly have slipped
this far, I don't care how many centuries have
elapsed.) They sang that crazy song about the three little fish
dancing a jig under the ice as they tromped across the
lumpy landscape of salt-encrusted grasses (I am imagining
a sort of Scandinavian moor here) toward the warm
hearth and stewpot that awaited. Louie, always the loudest,
croaking like a jackdaw as each fish counted backwards
to the beginning of time. But no one gave a shit. Blood

is thicker than harmonics. And when these robust, turnip-fed
farmer-Vikings shoved open the four-inch-thick
slab door (which was already slightly ajar) they gasped
and froze in their manured boots. An old woman
sat by the fire, stirring the stewpot, casting a walleyed
glance at the intruders. Eventually the family
began to thaw, mutter, shuffle cautiously along the edges
of the room. In time, the woman rose and
left – without a word spoken. Next week a cow died
and no one was surprised.

SECURED HEATED
STORAGE
IDEAL FOR FILES, ETC.
CALL: 390-3115

In December 2007, upon decree of a provincial court judge, Nanaimo's Red Zone was expanded by several orders of magnitude. It is now bounded by Fitzwilliam and Bastion streets on the north, and by Milton and Esplanade on the south. This is nearly forty blocks. Basically all of downtown Nanaimo. Previously it had been one block. To be banned from the Red Zone, one need not be tried and convicted of a crime but merely accused of one. The story ran in the paper, and nobody said a peep. Including me.

Heap of Songs

When my friend who is a crack addict was in an accident
and broke his leg in three places, the doctors couldn't set
the bone because it powdered to the touch—just heaps of old
songs, they muttered, scattering with each puff
of breath, each scrape of bowl, some vaguely human
deconstruction zone strewn with windblown notes and keen
unwound, shadow-surfing down the day

weightless

despooled strings

of

unsinging

dancing the

hErkY JerKy

in empty

space

till snagging on corners of brick, bistro
tables, patrons' hair
to be coveted, fought over
captured by house sparrows the following spring
and woven back to coherence

Tsunami

It wasn't much of a storm warning. Just a
glove on a stranger's hand—and I am mallet-smashed
by a whack of forgotten peptide chains
busting down the cellar door and clattering
past, claiming every loose fibre and rat-hole synapse
like a south seas typhoon after a seven-year
drought. They say it's in your head but my jellylegs
give out while some unseen paw fumbles
into my gaping chest to squeeeeeeeeze
bruising sun-ripened tomatoes till little rivulets
of V-8 juice gutter into the surrounding
crevices. I climb into my hip-waders and tie a length
of sturdy ganglia around my waist so I
won't be swept away as I venture forth to consult
the tape library upstairs. (If the answer is anywhere
that will be the place, although I cannot be sure
the collection has escaped flood
damage.) I grab a cassette that seems the right
size and shape, stuff it in the dripping
deck and hear it say: *Be mindful of your position*
on the time-space continuum
Which I take to mean "Be present" (although I could
just be hearing what I require or expect, yet I know
my collection pretty well so I think this is the intended
message). And we all dig what's coming
next—I must get into the basement where this insurgency

hatched and somehow shove my way
through the lofting tide and bobbing assault army
of my worse-than-useless possessions
to reach the far corner and throw the master
breaker before the next big wave crests and fricassees
the whole damn dump. No time to search
for my heavy-gauge lineman's gloves. Or your black
polar-fleece gloves that hugged your perfectly
angled T'ai Chi hands curved into tiger's
mouths down at the park as the sun climbed above
the fir trees, soft and furry with new snow. There's no time
for any gloves at all. I'm going in barehanded—
wish me luck.

What is that dead Danish cow doing in here stinking up the joint worse than the piss streams in the underpass? Its rotting corpse is four centuries gone, and on another continent. I keep bunting it out, but it lumbers back in late at night when my pipsqueak mind is snagged on facebook's barbed fence line. And why does my reanimated cow always bed down in the same spot? On the lee side of the poem about the woman trying to decapitate a parking meter. At least I know where to find it when I go to chase it out the next morning. Yet something about its placement, its persistence over time and space, its mangy flesh-dropped hide, sends bile rising to the back of my throat like when I found the dead raccoon behind my rain barrel and its tail came off in my hand as I carried it to the trash. If I were more fluent in Dead Cowese, perhaps I could decode what its glassy eyes and decaying pelt are trying to tell me. There is the stench of failure here. And it may be mine.

Walking to the Library

A kingfisher rips the blue off winter,
rattle-drops through alder fingerbones, strafes
the stiffened cut of day. My breath drifts up in

lazy lassos aiming for that silver dollar sun hidden
in a tin bucket sky. I clear the wind-bent cottonwoods
just past the Rimini Estates *(own a piece of nature*

downtown!) getting banged up on the back side of
Howard Johnson's and the bus depot. Last summer this
was still a brushy homeless campground, a forgotten

tangle of Himalayan blackberry and oceanspray, cryptic
hobbit trails twisting down to littered lip
of Millstone River—a kilter cardboard city

cobbled from flattened boxes, damp bedding, deck chairs,
blunt alcoves punched in scrubby thickets and abandoned
dreams. They are sleeping now

in the underpass (mostly), behind the concrete wall
on which the Island Highway balances as it spans
the river busting Nanaimo

in half. The overflow lies scattered
along the rest of the Scenic Harbourside Walkway
up to the ferry terminal, tastefully screened

behind boxwood hedging, stairwells, long
walls of memorial plaques dedicated to cherished
loved ones *(you always made us laugh...*

forever in our hearts...). And I start to wonder
about this underpass and its phalanx of blanketed
shopping carts lining the chain-link fence that keeps

our prized cruise ship tourists from splaying
down the riverbank to meet untimely
litigation. Some days the carts are parallel parked,

other days nose-in like dusty dozing horses tethered
to hitching posts outside Joe's Nickel Shave and
Rosie's Gold Nugget Saloon in some Hollywood

oater. There is an unspoken rule that safeguards
each cart from bedroll pirates, self-deputized
clean-up crews, bicycle police, bored teens *(you don't go*

messing with another man's buggy in these parts pardner,
not unless you want to see daylight through your belly).
This defacto shelter-slash-urinal has become a back-channel

drop site for the entire town's castaway sweaters, boots,
socks, plaid mufflers, winter coats, all carefully wrapped
in plastic and left on the cinder-block retaining wall for

whoever needs them most. When did we become a nation
of loose shopping carts? A nation clatter-bumping
through the night on six-inch wheels. A nation unlaced,

half-keeled, forever waiting on broad capstones. A nation
softly beating to the flux and thrum of great purpose
overhead. A nation asurge in returnable cans, shoulder-slung

sacks, a nation haphazard as broken teeth
defending the sandy backfill and pigeon-struck pillars
of cement cathedrals.

There is someone in my life who is no longer really there (even when I am staring at the loose curve of shoulder, lean nape of neck). But I keep him close so that his absence will continue to scrape away at the soft scab of my yearning and incompleteness. For if it were to heal over, hardening to a vague smudge marking the end of a reel, I am afraid the words will cease. And not just the words that appear to pertain to this person, but all the words. That is the downside of invincibility, of being too successful at sealing the container. You will likely staunch creative expression since this is technically a loss of jing. So I keep bleeding myself with memory leeches (under closely supervised conditions, mind you) so that I do not grow too strong. So that my outstretched arms cannot span so far that there is nothing left to reach.

1.

CATERPILLAR (OR LARVA) - Her first meal is often her own eggshell. As she grows, she will shed her inelastic skin 4-6 times. *(March 27, 2007)*

4.

EGGS - A single female can lay up to 1,600 eggs in her lifetime. Preferred substrates include recently grey-washed surfaces. *(May 21, 2008)*

The ubiquitous **Graffito urbanitus**, *common to both hemispheres, is an extremely hardy species resistant to nearly all known pests, killjoys and paint-rollers. This specimen was photo-documented over a 14-month period behind the Cambie in Nanaimo's designated Red Zone. The species is typically found clinging to concrete, brick, shiplap, steel and other vertical sidings, and exhibits a special affinity for dilapidated downtown cores.*

Life Cycle

2.

PUPA (OR CHRYSALIS) - During this quiescent phase the individual restructures herself. *(December 30, 2007)*

↓

3.

ADULT - The pupal skin splits open near the head to allow the newly formed concept to emerge and take flight. *(March 21, 2008)*

←

AGP

squat

tchook kuh kuh
tchook kuh kuh
tchook kuh kuh
tchook kuh kuh

this tangled tideline
of wads
of knotted waste
of lifes amalgam
of brasjeansplasticbagskleenexsweatersexplodedtampons
empty lighters jackets missing arms
socks absent shoes
shoes absent laces
this spewed up snake of thriftstore flotsam washing from room
to room to room in windowsmashed freight depot
fronting dockside railyard

tchook kuh kuh
tchook kuh kuh
tchook kuh kuh
tchook kuh kuh

these wads of damp
of done for
of gone
of lives tied off tied up tied out of sight
of anonymous lumpenkind

S
NAM
V
E

thalo blue spray bleeding
down concrete blocks
surrounded by outline of cross

WE TRYED AND LOST
ARE LIFES

more thalo blue bookended by cartoon syringes
the real ones scattered across dead sea
of scuffed linoleum (startled fingerlings flushed
from ammonia shadows)

tchook kuh kuh
tchook kuh kuh
tchook kuh kuh
tchook kuh kuh

the red zone
didn't work

they just came here instead
across esplanade

to jack wads into their flattened arteries and
thalo blue veins ripping
the nictitating membrane off the eyes
of the rest of us

tchook kuh kuh
tchook kuh kuh
tchook kuh kuh
tchook kuh kuh

take my photo and I'll chop your head off and
chuck it in the snowbank ya fuckin bitch!
I shot flotsam instead

KEEP OUT
I AM FELING REALY BAD

cardboard sign on blanket door
small slip of privacy
for photocopy nook
a shrouded tenant in each cell   15? 20?
desk drawers upside down in
paper tidepools file cabinets tipped
dreams tossed on slag heap above highline
every starfish drying to stardust
moon ceasing to pump leaving
ebb

without   flow

the red zone
didn't work

plywood is the cheapest fix
to seal this hive by sunday when the well flossed
public surges to scenic waterfront for shipboard tour of
coastal renaissance the largest double
ender in the world
free cookiescoffeephoto with six foot seagull in
captains uniform

the plywood
didn't work

it is time for new thinking
lets strap them to flatcars and keep them rolling forever
through this rat maze of catacombs left over from
coalmining days   *YES!*
our empty subterranean guts
will safeguard our precious minutemen of cultural
decay
must keep them invisible
untouchable
incurable
eternal

tchook kuh kuh
tchook kuh kuh
tchook kuh kuh
tchook kuh kuh

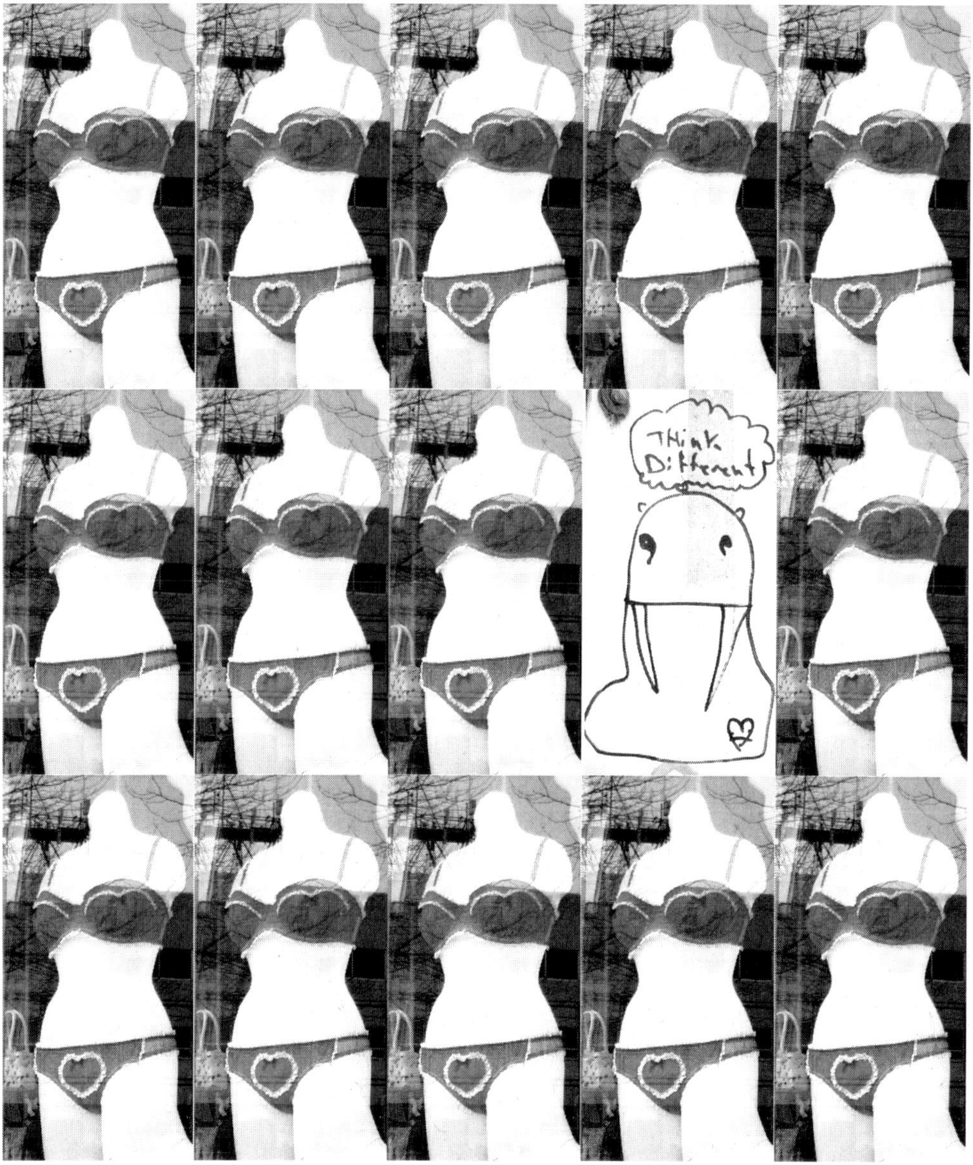
THink Different

Terra Incognita

This brain
was meant to be my offering
so I would not be thought a gate-crasher
at your garden party

I tried
to save you some
wrapping it carefully in saran
held aloft with toothpicks to preserve
the topping   But I got hungry
along the way

The years have gnawed
my impulse
control down to spotless
nubs (is this demyelination?)
I do not understand these crumbs
in my pocket
(are they poems?)

Please forgive me
for arriving
empty-handed   I won't
stay long and I promise to sweep up
any eggshells from unintended
hatchlings on my watch

It took me two days to recover from my first visit to the squat. My limbs were downed power lines dancing on tin roofs. My pulse surged and scattered like an alien tide. (Is this what it feels like to be tasered?) But which squat was I recovering from? The one across from Thrifty's, on the edge of the railyard? Or the one within, populated by engorged slabs of my own mortality, passion, shame, fraud – swollen fleshworms nodding aimlessly in their cinnabar chamber, blind as whips. I did not mean to rip the blanket door off this particular cubicle.

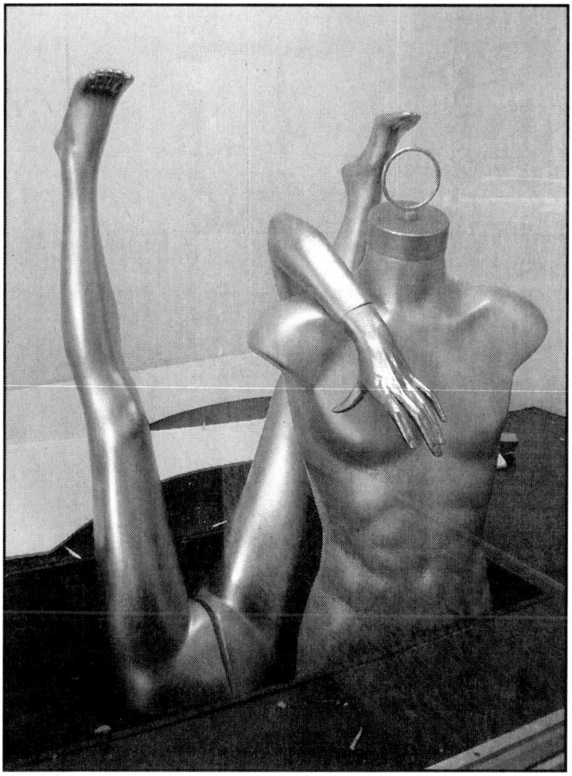

Working Theory

All knowledge is retrospective
self-reflexive, a puffed tin of
sardines gone off, a bloody head trauma waiting
to be washed raw, flushed, stuffed tight
with cool grey staghorn moss then sutured
shut by sentence fragments & dangling
particle colliders. I rode that

compound bus to the river bend
til I got busted with no ticket so I lept
rolled, tucked all the egg-beaters but still
lost my head (or was that my bed?)
the puffball thingie on top of
this himalayan rocksalt pillar (which will cure me
if I buy enough, free shipping for
kingsize) that I sleep in. I sleep standing
now since losing my puffball

so I can pillar-walk my pillow-talk.
Anything less would be sexy sheer
hypocrisy. And I can't stand hippopotamuses
like that. Neither can you, which you would
recall if you would ever wake up. China is a state
of mind. A self-induced coma, really.
Geography only exists to give our brainwaves
something to wipe their shaggy myelin-sheathed

egg-beaters with (which is why the best
maps are made from staghorn moss). Du bist immer
in China now, that place that is as far away
as a heartbeaten busboy can go without
leaving the planterbox altogether, which we do not yet
know how to do
at least not in a permanent
wave solution. Which sperm-shoots us back
to the instigating theory of knowledge &
its construction. Building starts

are up this quarter. The 2010 Olympics
will suck the world in all its rawness
up the bright green bunghole of Vancouver Island
where each Tilley hat can read Sartre
& Ghandi & Shakespeare on shithouse walls
at the riverside bus depot while taking a free
dump (that some world somewhere
down the linoleum will pay for – but not us, not
with our hammers swinging, our concrete
pouring, our 4x8 magic plywood rides soaring o'er
the tired graveyard of decaying shopping
carts, their encrusted skeletons rising
like rampikes in this upthrust urban forest
at low tide). Even the Chinese
are expected to come. Maybe I will see you

button-wedged among them, flattened
like an off sardine. I will snip you free
so we can sneak away & pillar-walk
our pillow-talk up the middle
of the Millstone River in the middle
of the night beneath a middlesex moon
skewered on a stag's sheer
hornswoggle. We were born on the ledge

of Knowing. We will make love-
ly new maps. We will take our place
beneath the highway cool & grey
where our twoness will remain, will provide
a (relatively) safe planterbox for all
the dangling sentence fragments
to sleep behind in their self-reflexive
freedom.

WE ONLY BECOME
WHAT WE ARE
BY THE RADICAL &
DEEP-SEATED REFUSAL
OF THAT WHICH OTHERS
HAVE MADE OF US
JEAN-PAUL SARTRE
AMP
WAS
HERE

When I was fifteen, a juvenile court judge banned me from Coos County, Oregon. He had apparently grown weary of my encore performances. His order stipulated that I was to be picked up and jailed if sighted anywhere within the county line. Coos County is 1,600 square miles. The ban remained in place until I turned eighteen. If he could have extended it into my senior years, I am sure he would have. My mother, who taught college English in Coos Bay, quit her job and moved to Eugene where she had no job.

How could I have forgotten all this until now? What happens to those who are rendered invisible by law but do ***not*** *forget? Do they grow transparent until phone poles and hubcaps show right through them?*

Immaculate Conception

tumble of green blanket
caught on bramble ledge, shopping cart
sleeps in streambed

six a.m.—still dark
with winter when morning shift starts
at homeless shelter

rubber gloves wipe down
sleeping pads using ten percent
bleach solution

coffee and eggs
toast too—hot shower, dry clothes
then out the door

pigeon coo lullaby
droplets kiss sand in rumble cocoon
of underpass

small dog in plaid coat
trots past sleeping bag, leaves frosty
stitch of paw prints

fourth week of snow
and only the unitarians open
their doors

old sweaters and coats
left in underpass, christmas wrapped
in plastic bags

dark waters flood temple
wash away spent dreams, god thunders
overhead

body found in barsby
park, police do not suspect
foul play

no two alike, pristine
as unpinned stars dropping silently
to flux of river

GOD HAVE MERCY
ON MY Soul

This, I now believe, is why he spits and turns away when I speak. Why he shields himself within a flock of chi gong zombies who occasionally startle and stampede, thus explaining the hoof-shaped bruises along his torso some mornings (I am speculating here). He understands the magnitude of his role as Muse, knows precisely how many shrunken heads are needed to write a book, transform a city, undam a stagnant sea.

cloud-
popped
she
began
to
rain
友

Leavings

You were blowing winter
all summer long out the shiny brass
bowl of your saxophone
down at the park You were blowing
so hard your lungs
came out at the end after all the
hailstorms and ice dams
and snowbanks that swallowed up
stop signs
(and here of all places
in what is supposed to be
a temperate zone the banana
belt of Canada)
Their pink crowns pushing
out of your polished
bowl your inverted liberty
bell your golden cornucopia of
silence giving birth at last to
something alive
and self-defining They swelled
to cumulonimbus size
then drifted off along the leaden
vault of sky These two pink dirigibles
defying snow-laden air
and your festering fear and
our shared construct of gravity Basically

just defying all modes
of incarceration in general
whether Newtonian or
quantum in outline Two cotton
candy zeppelins on a reconnaissance
mission seeking a brighter
astral body to occupy
or simply making a run for it Weightless
as an empty room filled with every
possibility They were always
the best part of you Now just two pink
specks
I watched until they winked
goodbye

Nocturne

To the untrained eye, every night is a mirror likeness
of its predecessor, rising threadlong from scattered
filings left by day's departed outline, dark magnet swallowing

all the odd angles, forgotten plans, remnant bodies
of thought, greyscaling those last stabs
at determinacy (which never had a beggar's

chance), exhaling them in coarse westerly strands that sweep
tatters of Canada geese and gulls up the mouth
of an outpouring estuary, against the stubborn thrust

from our indifferent riparian culture, depositing stray feathers
and the city's chaff on stiff hassocks of
salal. But beneath such pitchy protocol (this yaw and toss

of upheaved social codes and insufficiently practiced
team breakout patterns), hums a plasticine
brain, shapeshifting, restringing high-tension

cable, gauging future trends, discarding the abandoned
stations (those useless wasters! no train has come this way
in centuries) through apoptosis, hence the ambulances

atop the riverbank park at the end of my street when night
recedes and the morning charcoals its decisive boundary
around whatever is left behind.

Pristine

But this one is my favourite: You are really Pao P'u Tzu, the legendary Master Who Preserves His Pristine Simplicity. And you have amnesia. (One forgets a lot in 1,700 years. Just last week I forgot the scissors I went out to buy to make this book. Even had them in my hand before I saw the garden whirlygigs. Had to drive back to Dollarama but it was closed. Creativity postponed due to globalization and aging.) This explains a great deal—your stewpot, my braising, these fleshy tracts of memory falling from the bone, confusion vaporized, taking flight as a lungful of ruby-crowned kinglets rushing past teeth and tongue, collapsing my chest so I can populate it anew with species of my choosing. Is it soup yet? Is this the elixir? Is it? (Our relationship was never what it seemed.) *Having features seek the featureless.* You printed it on your club T-shirts so we wouldn't forget. But knowledge is more than neural networks alight with peptides. All of which means that in the end it will fall to me to hide your body (leaving perhaps your kung fu shoes and broadsword in some not-too-hard-to-discover location, maybe under the rhododendrons by the pavilion) to preserve your status as a corpse-free Immortal.

友
slugs
only
appear
slow

I have begun making weathergrams and hanging them in the riverside park near my house, where the homeless sleep.

Weathergram: a message rendered on a strip of paper (old shopping bags are best) then tied to a tree (think: language as leaf, as fruiting body, as seedpod husk) where it will weather with the changing seasons until it ultimately unravels and slips away on a current of water or air. Or perhaps just falls to the earth and is re-absorbed.

Mimotype

(a form which resembles another in
general shape but not genetic makeup)

Yellow as the aspen leaf drifting to earth
Yellow as the cat-skidder lurching up hills

Perfect as the killdeer eggs hidden in plain sight
Perfect as the crankcase oil dribbled on white sand

Crumpled as the bracken unfurling each spring
Crumpled as the beer cans hurled from diesel-stinking cabs

Flat as the red-winged blackbird's black eye
Flat as the real estate sign that went up last night

Still as the absent dawn chorus on forestless slopes
Still as the backhoe surveying broken morsels of the day

In the fall, they bulldozed the vacant lot at the end of my street to make it more attractive to prospective land developers. ("A guy likes to see what he's getting into," I once read in a women's advice column extolling the benefits of pubic shaving.) For three years, I had traipsed through this brushy half-acre every single day on my way downtown without once being aware of the homeless encampment screened behind tangles of alder and buddleia, tucked up against a concrete retaining wall for shelter from the wind and wet. After it was flattened, I poked through the abandoned furnishings: collapsible lawn chairs, burnt tin pot, rubbermaid tote for table, pine shelf unit lashed to rebar to keep it high and dry, loaded with boots, sneakers, platform heels, blue jeans, can opener, chipped plates, Canucks sweatshirt. No one ever returned. Months later the stuff was still there, so I took the shelf unit home, painted it purple and put it in my greenhouse.

Next spring, I staged the Urban Eyes Art Exhibition. It filled two downtown galleries, transformed to streetscapes, with the work of 52 artists and architects. I wanted to know what a city built from art would look like. I found out. Everybody came. But did they see?

COMMUNITY SERVICES
BE AN ORGAN DONOR
GIVE YOUR
HEART TO
JESUS

Gates of the City

This is the garden

This is the scattering of fallen pears
    browning in long grass

This is the closer glance, the tour bus
    kodak moment of the digitally captured herd
        asnooze on the savannah

These are the mounds of almost-
    life waiting for their time, over-ripened fetal
        curls quietly fermenting in spew of tailpipes

This is the new hope
    centre rising as leviathan across the highway

These are the jaws unhinging, swinging
    wide to passively consume the motile

These are the fourmilliondollar twentybeds
    offered freely to those who do not swear or have
        "bad conversations"

This is the little prayer
they must all say, have all been saying since
residential school days, small hands knotted
in fetal curls, in captured herds, their unhinged
hearts quietly fermenting in spew
of charity

This is the scattering of fallen
pears browning in long grass

These are the mounds of almost-life
waiting for their time

This is the garden

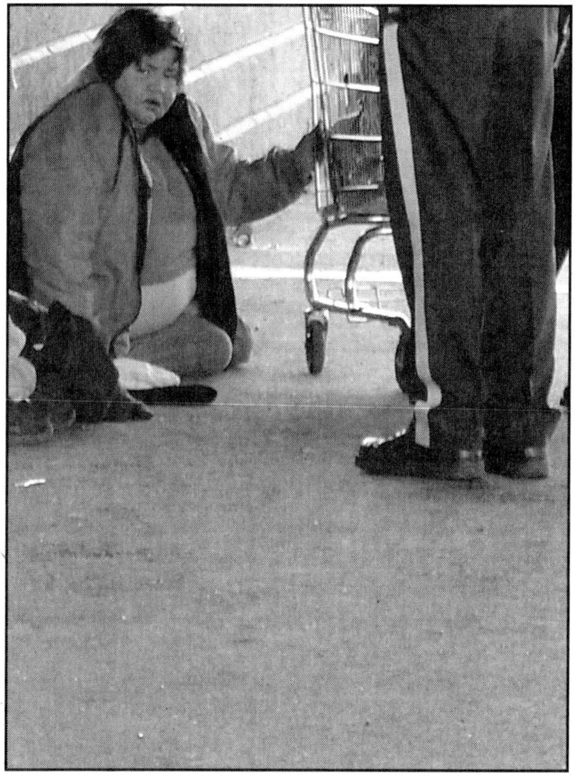

The Invention of Language

g I g
s HAVE s
g AN g
s URGE s
2
de FORM ed
g A g
s WORD s
g A g
s TRAIT s
2
s LEEVE s
g A g
s TONE s

d I d
s HAVE s
s INK s
2
s PRINT s
s IT s
g A g
s LIP s
2
s TOUT s
s IT s
g A g
s TOOL s
2
s CARVE s
s IT s
s IN s
g AN g
s OAK s

d I d
s EVEN s
s HAVE s
g AN g
s EAR s
2
g UTTER IN g
2

s NOW s
d I d
s WILL s
re SEARCH er
4
d A d
s WORD s

HELLO!
My name is...
IN8 4CE

smart bomb

I am a smart bomb
I am a smeared burn
I am a startled turn
I am a turtle dove
I am a girl in love
I am a title search
I am a purchase price
I am a pride of lions
I am a proud american
I am a propeller fin
I am a fingerling
I am a funny uncle
I am a seared lung
I am a sealed breech
I am a borrowed code
I am a walmart toaster
I am a talking stick
I am a steel cocoon
I am a depleted thought
I am a monsanto peach
I am a bearded frog
I am a firmament
I am a yearning heart
I am a yellow hearse
I am a retro virus
I am a jailer's curse
I am a target taker
I am a barred owl
I am a tick tock
I am a fallen log
I am a fiddled book
I am a shift in flight
I am a swift retort
I am a sworded ox
I am a stock market
I am a smart bomb

WE ARE MORE THAN WAR BLED DRY, EPICENTER ASLAUGHTER
WE ARE MORE THAN WARBLED DRY EPIC, ENTER AS LAUGHTER
WE ARE MORE

in8 4ce

I have no crew   I am a rogue
agent lobbing wordbombs along the low-slung
scabrous belly of our collective body Sometimes
a motivating factor in stampedes and other
herd maneuvers   I'm an urban
plastic surgeon remodelling the skin of this
declining milltown swelled with mallbloat Let's make it pop
and sing and splay the rat-torn epic of
late capitalism in fluorescent orange This is the language
of rejoinder in a grilled cheese world encased
in its own sloppy grease The language of things
that cannot be said Of things
that cannot be permitted to be true The language of
unerasure (no matter how many times
it is obliterated) The language
of being
of existence
of We Are Here   These are the rules
of engagement writ fast and
ripped (with shoe polish if need be)

When I was fifteen and thrown into
a coos bay jail over a long
weekend for some dubious adolescent
infraction I left my mark carving sergeant kaufman
has crabs into the scaling greenwashed

plaster with a fork held back from my salisbury
steak tv dinner three hours earlier My first samizdat poem
went unnoticed until after my release when
my mother got a call from the police station telling her
to bring me back down so I could repaint
the cell They were all surprisingly
friendly The man who brought me the tray and roller
gave me a lit cigarette For some reason
I was embarrassed to tell him I didn't smoke But he
could guess by my choking

PUSH - POUSSEZ
PULL-TIREZ
All other destinations / Toutes autres destinations
To Buy Crack Cross Street

squat (postscript)

spew of powdered stars
mouthful of locks with no
keys, boundless

herds of rocks—hobbled, slurping
dustbowls, grazing hardened
thought, wasted
as three-legged atoms, as frozen oceans, crashed

as wave, vacant
with stampede, with gone, with
done for

PAULSON

I know what it is to lose a voice. I misplaced one for eight years (although I now think it ran off in search of that ultimate plate of nachos, or perhaps just a landscape with fewer boundaries). My voice turned up one morning in the underpass with a lumpy garbage sack slung over its shoulder. I was walking to the seaside park for my daily T'ai Chi and didn't recognize it at first. It just looked like every other rumpled mound slumped on the capstones. But when I met its glance, I knew. And it knew I knew. It reached into its sack and offered me a poem for a cup of coffee and a warm room. This seemed a fair trade, and I was glad to have my voice back after all these years alone—even in its fragmented state. I was sure I could mend it, give it a shave, stretch it out to feature-length articles again, maybe even another nonfiction book or two. But every time it reached into its sack, all it handed me was a poem.

One night while my voice slept (purring like an air compressor), I crept into the kitchen and opened the bag. There must be a head-knocking exposé in here somewhere, some killer investigative piece on deep integration or child labour or the government sell-off of our rivers. But I was wrong. It's poems all the way.

Leonard's Ladder

Amid

wandering thoughts
he knew deep down that

laundering thoughts
was no use because

laundering shorts
never cured anyone of anything real, not
gout or VD or depression—it was far more
complicated (and likely involved
some pharmaceutical conspiracy and the
spin-doctoring of Burson-Marsteller). He began

pondering shirts
knowing all the while
that clothes do not make the manhole
in much the same way that

pandering hurts
because it cuts the truth out of
your knockwurst like a

panhandler's curse
knife-thrown at your departing
indifference, catching an exposed
scapula, maybe

puncturing fascia
that wasn't really holding up its end
anyway, just slacking off with all those
other cornfed body parts, so many clueless
ruminants seeking nothing more than a
flock to belong to, a shepherd to lead them,
a song to bleat in three-part harmony.
They're such

fungible fascists
every one, slumbering in the braindome,
snug as

recumbent bananas
in their unpeeled and freshly sponge-mopped
cerebellums

pregnant as cancer
stalking unwitting earthworms and other
free spirits with their

dollar-store sledgehammers
made in special enterprise zones where
euphemisms of all races and creeds live side
by side, strumming banjos by the
levee, leading long and happy lives. And he
wondered about all the

wandering thoughts

that had fallen off clifftops—not all at once,
of course, but over many centuries, and it
occurred to him that these plummeting
thought-rocks could account for a certain
percentage of unexplained deaths in
otherwise healthy people and livestock. He
took great comfort from this realization
and decided he could improve
his odds immediately by moving someplace
flat like Saskatoon.

OPEN
MONEY MAXX
CASH LOANS
PARKING IN REAR

Growth Industry

and the trimmers make twenty bone an hour
which beats poetry all to hell   my pay level approximates
that of the bluejeaned hookers on albert giving
five dollar blowjobs which wont even buy a new
used pair of nikes at the thrift shop down the block although
an industrious set of lips or keypounding
fingertips could probably spin that into trimmer pay
just four suckoffs/poems an hour   still
thats hard fucking work   were talking stuff of
chain gangs pickaxing rockpiles sweating their wrongly
accused whipstung brains out under a sweltering
climatechanged sun bracing for the next lash from some sadistic
turnkey with a mother complex while those fucking
slackass trimmers are lounging hydroponic poolside under
ten thousand watts of halogen styling in their designer shades
their every want sated before it even stumblefoots into
their cannabissoaked craniums   free beer pizza smokes
name your pleasure just keep cutting that leaf away from bud
their latex gloves so resinous gumstuck theyll be packing a
weeklong ross rebagliati buzz when theyre done   yes
even right through the rubber sheathing   the only wrinkle is
they cant leave till the whole crop is cut theyre so skunked they
might as well wear tshirts saying growop trim crew
follow me home   and nobody wants that
but so fucking what   i mean who wants to leave a party
where youre paid to get greased   does life get any sweeter?

which is why i am contemplating a career change   im gonna
break on through that semencaked alphabetsoup ceiling
keeping me and all my cocksucking poemscribbling sisters
down   im gonna grab the brass ring
grab me a gig trimming with the guys slapping backs
swapping raunchy jokes talking about bellhousings and
twin carbs and cv joints
i got my shades
i got my latex gloves
i got my henckels cutting like james bond razorblades
so shove over tokeheads   poemgirl is coming around to play

WANTED

For crimes against walls, lampposts, real estate signs, dumpsters, downspouts, plywood, railway switchboxes, flatcars and other defenceless blank slates sheeted in tranquil grey, beige, taupe, charcoal, non-absorptive silver or the hardened porridge of form-poured concrete raked tight as ribbed condoms on a tribeful of New Brutalist monoliths ice-picking a colourless sky with no dimension whatsoever, for crimes against conformity, coherence, deference to authority, collectively accepted meaning, truth, beauty, laws of gravity, in fact the entire Newtonian canon, for crimes against a pacified sea of hollow craniums sloshing gently along the hard-packed sands of a made-in-china beach leaving an eggshell necklace as each wavelet retreats with its dollarstore spoils, for crimes against the vacant eyes of a lobotomy nation, against vacancy overall in each of its self-replicating disguises, for capsizing the sinking lifeboat, for wearing her heart on a tree, for daring to think backwards, span a gap, sync up, tie a knot or two, for being a Human Doing

blueprints

day by day the city structured itself
around blueprints left the night before...

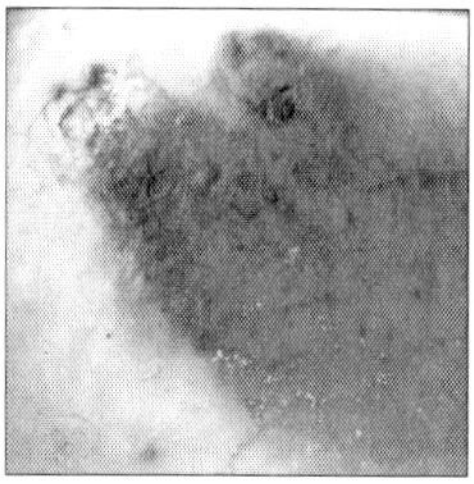

and when the architects were outlawed
their schematics skinned over in grey
the city forgot itself, became flaccid cells absent dna
absent the germ of possibility, thus reverting
to the original algorithm for calculating hum spatter
of bell-rung air

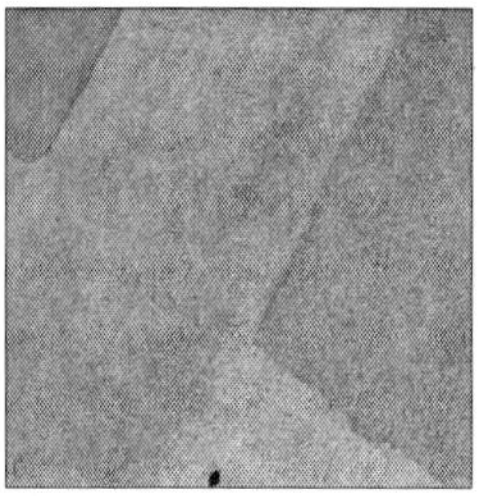

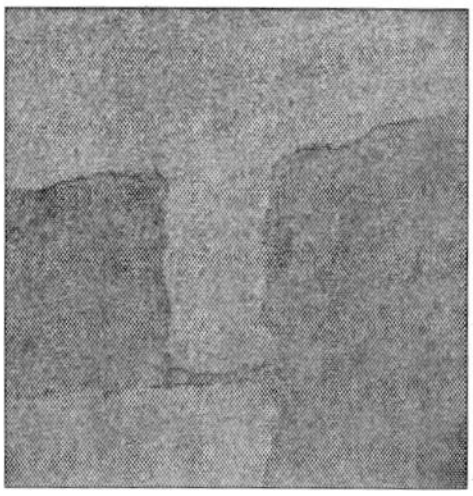

I can no longer discern where the political ends and the personal begins. The deeper I push into this swollen red midden of hidden box springs and open books, the more my own flesh burns. I watch my thirsting heart burst on a brick wall above a shopping cart. I feel the Millstone sloshing through my veins. (Have the salmon returned? Has he?) I cannot separate my obsessions. They are feasting on me in a great banquet hall with much thigh slapping and guffaws. How can I possibly be vast enough to sustain them all?

What keeps drawing me to this shadowplay of squat, tagging, underpass? Is it the power of bearing witness? The drive to signify? The chance to lose myself in this ragged landscape of decline? Or am I just another addict in pursuit of my slippery (but fabulously well-muscled) Muse?

IF THE DOORS OF PERCEPTION
WERE CLEANSED, THINGS WOULD
APPEAR TO MAN AS THEY TRULY ARE
INFINITE

Inner Sanctum

After the dunes have sifted away, after the hours
and minutes have fallen off
the clockface, the hash marks off the
yardstick, after some half-dozen cultural revolutions
have gone cartwheeling across the night
sky, when it becomes clear that no one is coming
to fetch her, she will rise
from her satin bench in the fur-lined
anteroom and amble (or perhaps it is more of a
saunter—the salient point here is that
she will not exhibit the halting rigidity born of fear
and apprehension) into the Great
Hall (this label is merely a narrative contrivance
for the sake of creating some mise-en-scène so that we may
comfort ourselves with faux comprehension
pretending to know what is happening, what this journey
is about) through a meat curtain strung across
a plaster arch (a vernacular style suggestive
of 1930s architecture, if that is of any help). She will know
it is a meat curtain (yes, I googled it too and that is
indeed what it means: *labia minora,* yet this was the image
that clung to me this morning as I coursed the waking
cusp of dream... my own barefoot passage through suspended
foldings of raw beef) and not strings of hand-rubbed
jade (the best we can hope for is that the massing of
relevant data might eventually sink us to the bottom

of the well) by the electron haze of houseflies
and the slip-tongue kisses—sticky, damp, sweet—suction-fitting
to her shoulders, collarbone, breasts,
thighs (she will be naked, you see, having off-loaded
in the antechamber) as she sweeps on by.

And I believe that if I write long enough, I will arrive at an answer, at something that passes for understanding. I will feel myself return to the solid state. Shapes will rise up from the slurry of tidal sand, will fabricate patterns, stake land claims. But it will cost me. The invisible lattice caging the wave whose hollow I have been surfing at right angles to the ocean's advance will collapse like last night's dreams. Oddly, to forestall knowing is to prolong coherence.

Set pieces for the Coliseum scene

✓ The aging elephants on aching legs.

✓ The trill of soothsayers from white-stained vault.

✓ The weary columns holding highway aloft.

✓ The press of graffiti crowding up damp wall.

✓ The strew of beer caps, plastic spoons, blankets
spread to dry.

✓ The spent exhaust wafting out tattered mouth
of Millstone at low tide.

✓ The snowmelt slanting across asphalt path.

✓ The man supine, hands stacked on heart, serene as sacrifice,
as sleeping beauty.

✓ The veer of strollers, the growl of midget dogs, the clatter
of shopping carts.

✓ The click of a digital camera.

✓ The whiff of spirits and brine.

✓ The woman climbing the sandbank for a better angle.

✓ The hack of internal combustion.

✓ The tethering of tour buses.

✓ The restless gladiators pigeon-perched on capstones halfway
down the nave, glancing, turning away.

I want to read these poems in the underpass, downstream from my weathergram park. Homeless people roost here too in their hibernaculum behind the wall, while the Island Highway mutters them to sleep. When one of the Leonards I have gotten to know slept alone and out in the open last month, he awoke to three men beating him. He spent the next two weeks on life support. Safety comes in clusters, barricades, invisibility, which can be scarce out here on the world's final reach. I want to feel the sound of my words echoing in this scrawled cathedral, bouncing off the pigeon-strafed vault. I want to learn if utterance can change the thing being spoken about. Will these mastodon columns release their hallowed souls? Will Leonard's mashed-in nose become a cactus-dotted box canyon sheltering a secret village? One never knows these things if poetry won't leave the haven of the coffeehouse, won't stand on the precipice, wind-smacked, tongue-kissing the infinite.

Television Interview in the Underpass
(for National Poetry Month)

there
that dog-size
gap
they dug this tunnel
in the sand
to sleep
behind the wall
each night they
elbowwalk
& bellycrawl beneath
bright blaze
of salmon mural
collapsing
gritty lungs
tight as
sailorfists
vestigial legs twist
& squeeeeeeze it
under
firecracker riptide
whipsaw fishtails banging
along night's
chill length
of concrete
toward beer &

winestore
spawning ground
red crush of
ripe persimmons gone
to bloodied
pulp with
shredded fins
their golden
eyes aflood
afire
afear
a dull thrust
a must push forward
the rush
to reach the shoal
dig the redd
spread the milt
& seed
spill it all before
the final
guttering

WILD CAT!....

Just another dead cow out grazing in our cosmological fallacies

On nights when sleeps drags its dopey
heels my mind is a ball
of kitchen string unspooling to find
the true sequence for these poems—who stays
who gets thrown aside
creating my own private Red Zone so this
book does not become a town dump
of poetry So some reader might actually want to
live here (We usually start with a noble
plan or at least a practical one) Half-blinded

by winter sun I am standing in a field of ripe
parking meters while a dead cow ambles down the
rows grazing the fattened heads off listing poles
I know the cow is dead by the Xs on her
eyes Blue bottle caps spill out the slobbery sides of
the dead cow's maw to form a watercourse streaming
down the blacktop
And I know this is the Kokanee River
because the Kokanee Brewing Company makes those
bottle caps And I am thinking how pretty this
sapphire swath smashing

across the black tar And I am laughing at the voracious
dead cow And I am guessing I have dropped off
and am dreaming

or this could be another dopamine spike
(I have been dosing myself with lecithin and
bee pollen and velvet bean) since these are the only
times when I know anything and I seem to
know an awful lot right now The mind is always reaching

for connection welding seams on the night
sky to forge epics and character flaws for the stars and fallen
meteors
so we know who to blame for dead farm animals
soft real estate markets
urban tumbleweeds
a machine winding down
because superstition is less painful
than gazing directly at complexity with the naked
mind And my aching mouth

stretches wide
becomes a slobbering maw
releasing an exodus of blood-fed poems scrawled
on soggy matchbooks that were clinging to my quilted
guts beside the train tracks their wet wings folded tight They burst
into flight this scatter of cardboard corpuscles
this big bang of Painted Lady
butterflies I think I see their pattern
but I could still be
dreaming

Tic Tac Truth

after Schopenhauer

All truth passes through three stages...

first
it is ridiculed

second
it is violently
opposed

third
it is accepted
as self-evident

first
it is ridiculed

second
it is violently
opposed

third
it is accepted
as self-evident

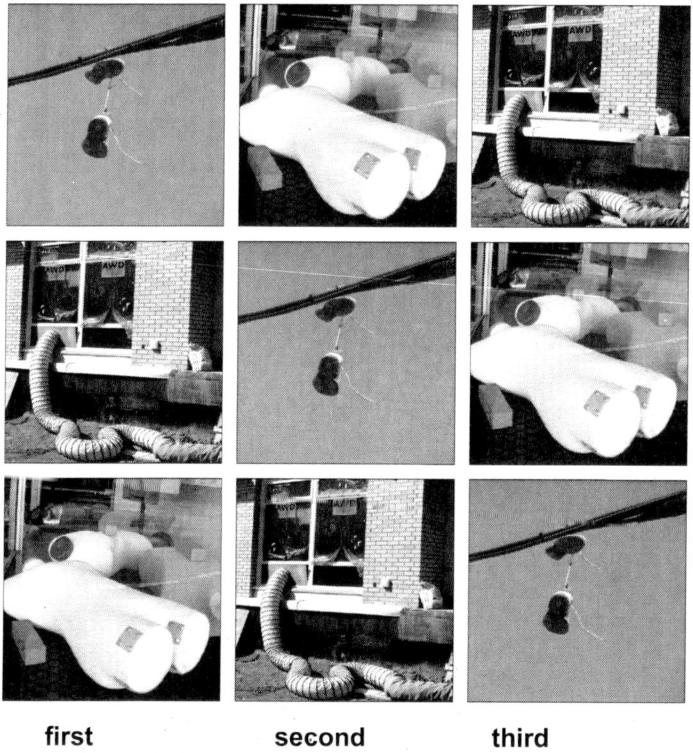

first
it is ridiculed

second
it is violently
opposed

third
it is accepted
as self-evident

first
it is ridiculed

second
it is violently
opposed

third
it is accepted
as self-evident

The secret is to know when you are truly lost. The mind is very clever, always plotting reference points, drawing schematics, charting a course. When it senses itself slipping into a shield of fog, it will throw out a deep-sea anchor to control drift so that when the fog lifts, the mind will not be far from its last known coordinates. This is the worst possible outcome. The fog is an opportunity to let everything go. Throw it all overboard. No one will see. Start with the anchor chain. Unbolt it from the deck.

underpass redux

I have spent too much time
among fools and thieves and overlords
I do not have enough words
to feed them all
Their profit-to-loss ratios have neglected to factor
structural collapse when too many
lattes are sloppy-stacked on a base of
rotting meat
The well while very deep does have a bottom
and everybody knows

When a well is being lined with stone
it cannot be used till the work is done

Return me now to the truth
of the underpass
That reclining well tucked up for the night
a night with no end
a night force-fed by the beer & wine store across the parking lot
a night populated by a cityful of Native men named Leonard
by a skyful of stars gone supernova when I arrive
Telling me I am gorgeous
Telling me they love my hair
Telling me how good it is to see me again
Telling me they can get me a free fish down at the docks
Have I ever tasted honey-smoked sockeye

or dungeness crab cooked in a pot on the beach?
Lets go haul up the traps!

Return me now to the underpass
with a chisel-tip sharpie and wandering heart
so I can spend this long night lining
our well with poems

Urban Getaway

The City was tired
like a man on death row or a newborn foal—tired of
waiting, of being legless, nameless, tongue-scraped by
alien forces.

The City wanted to start over
strike out, see the world, be roseate spoonbills
scissoring dark lagoons, taste donkeys gone to market
along the ravelling hem of the Sahara, know the
difference between past and present tense.

The City consulted the stars
It brought out elderly bronze tools hidden in refugee
camps of broken pencils by the duck pond. It spent
several centuries calculating tangents and cosines and
parabolic arcs, working like a cookstove or a clawfoot
tub—sleepless, hair-mussed, thirsty for hope. When the
formula was complete,

The City whispered the internal secrets
to all its constituent parts. The secrets were spider fists
acquiring tiny targets, hissing softly in meteorological
code that if overheard by invading soldiers would be
mistaken for impending snowfall.

The City let the plan unspool
like a slack gut of stagnant water crawling out to sea
in search of birth mother. We leave tonight,

The City gassed off
when they are sleeping. There will be no room for
supplies or provisions of any kind—no rucksacks,
coleman lanterns, stolen kisses, pup tents,
touchstones, quantum entanglements. Not even
your potholes or condom hollows or other vacant
spaces. We must all walk out naked, lighter than
hydrogen, or we will never get away... The parts
shivered, shot furtive glances, nodded like cars
backfiring, street-cleaners whisking cold curbs, hot
grease singing in swollen dumpsters. No discussion
was needed. When the sun went down, the
boundaries blurred and

The City drifted to the ledge
shepherding its soundless parts, obedient as a shorn
herd of silicon chips or a flock of rebar encased in
blind faith. Or maybe cheezwhiz. One by one each
cannon-balled into the chasm—chin tucked, shoulders
hunched, knees clasped to sunken chest, rusty
testicles plunging headlong, expelling last breath in a

smudge of confusion, just a small parting gift to the
occupying troops.

And The City was never seen again
although on sunny days, vague clusters of miasma
leave fuzzy shadows on the footprint of the former
site. Rumour has it The City may have reformulated
itself into white dwarfs and red giants in the winter
skies, which astrophysicists now know are actually
reflections of glistening fish guts wrapped tight as
shrunken cowhide at the centre of the earth.

Night Ride

We are driving down a road at night. It is very dark. There are no streetlights or houselights or tail lights. Or even any starlights overhead. Not a pinprick of photons to illuminate our journey beyond the wedge of our headlights. At least we have those, revealing swatch of pavement dead on, occasionally crosscut by blur of jackrabbit. Or maybe hyena. Now bounded by pairs of vitreous reflectors. And we reminisce (in voices we hope are carefree) about the practice of Mexican truck-drivers hugging cliffside highways at night with no headlights, claiming to see better without them. And we reminisce (in those still breezy voices) about southern France, where the drivers honk and wave fists if your headlights are white and not soothingly civilized amber. And we do not think we are in Mexico or France right now. But we cannot be certain. And the streaks of fur and claw flashing across our short-stopped wedge are getting harder to identify. One looks like a treble clef, another like string theory. We calculate probabilities, flowchart causality, redouble our commitment to carefree vocal tones. We do not mention the deteriorating road—now bumpy, now dirt, now grass, now a single fading chalk line scoring blackness. We are almost there.

Midnight Manifesto of a Chisel-tip Sharpie

Write it where it hasn't been written before (location!
location! location!)

Write it with risk or it is worthless

Write it in a language not yet invented, a language
comprehensible only to stem cells

Rise up and seize the tools of production—scrap of roofing
felt, tin cans, chain of dandelions, a sidelong glance

Do not engage herd-brain (it will only take you down the
road more traveled)

Do not collapse the wave function (unless you know how
to restore it)

Emote soon emote often—polls open 24/7

Ask not what Realism can do for you but what you can do
to subvert it, to eat its bright orange heart being power-
washed off trees in city parks

Irony is the shortest distance between foreground and
background—every true journey starts with one step remove
(faux journeys usually start with some cheap low-cut image
in come-fuck-me shoes)

Coherence is over (pick one: rated, trusted, coveted)

Diaspora is good for the universal soul (think mud puddles,
think big bang, think orders of magnitude)

We are more than subject-verb-predicate

We are more than a governing device

We are more than war bled dry, epicenter aslaughter

We are more than warbled dry epic, enter as laughter

We are more

Only
a city
is big enough
to hold this

I cannot
begin

to understand the secret

Workings
of
Stars

or your
heart

MAMBO
PIZZA
TAKE OUT
Light
shushing
cross
galaxies

GREYHOUND
GREYHOUN
Blood
Shushing
Past Valves

PALACE HOTEL
THE PALACE HOTEL
COLD BEER & WINE OFF SALES
flooding Chambers of

my
Vacant
mind

interstellar
riptide
sucked

under
Ventricular
Frequencies

dust stirred
plucked

feel me
hum